Saving Capitalism

by Robert B. Reich

Key Takeaways, Analysis & Review

By Instaread

Please Note

This is a key takeaways and analysis.

Table of Contents

OVERVIEW

Saving Capitalism: For the Many, Not the Few by Robert B. Reich examines the intersection of economics and politics in order to make sense of income inequality and wealth disparity in the 21st century United States of America.

The free market has been used to mask the reality of how big money, such as Wall Street, large corporations, and wealthy individuals, manipulate the market to their benefit, distributing wealth upwards at the expense of US working and middle classes. The real choice is not between a mythical free market and a demonized big government, but between a market designed to enhance the wealth of a minority at the top and a market designed to benefit the majority of US citizens.

The current economic and political system is creating a growing divide in US society between moneyed interests who fix the rules and everyone else who suffers the consequences. This state of affairs is not only economically unsustainable, but also politically dangerous, a threat to the functioning of US democracy. The only way to alter the status quo is for the majority to become informed, organized, and motivated to act. The majority must regain influence over the rules of the market in order to counteract the power of moneyed interests and reestablish an economy of widespread prosperity. It is not a matter of having more or less government, but of deciding who the government is really for and organizing the market accordingly.

IMPORTANT PEOPLE

Robert Reich: Robert Reich is a political and economic theorist and professor at the University of California, Berkeley. He served in the administrations of Presidents Ford, Carter, and Clinton.

John Maynard Keynes: An English economist born in 1883, Keynes is considered one of the most influential economists of the 20th century and the founder of modern macroeconomics. His school of thought, which challenged the tenets of neoclassical economics, is known as Keynesian economics.

Thomas Paine: One of America's founding fathers, Paine was an activist, political philosopher, and revolutionary. He authored influential pamphlets, including *Common Sense* and *Agrarian Justice*.

Key Takeaways

1. There is no such thing as the free market.

2. It is no coincidence that those who praise the free market are the moneyed interests who benefit most from this system.

3. Economic and political power are deeply connected. As moneyed interests gain dominance over the economy, they increase their influence over government, which in turn allows them to continue growing their wealth and entrenching their economic power.

4. The influence of the wealthy on the economy and politics undermines the trust on which capitalism depends. Lack of trust further damages the political and economic system as people become cynical, avoid reasonable financial risks, and start cheating in order to get by.

5. The notion that people earn what they are worth is a fallacy as it disregards the political institutions that define the market and determine worth. It also encourages

people to think there is nothing they can do to improve their situation.

6. The increasing power and influence of America's upper class has come at the expense of the declining power of the working and middle classes. The main problem is not economic, but political.

7. The growing divide in US society is not between Republicans and Democrats, but between the establishment and everyone else, the wealthy and the struggling majority. Ordinary people must establish a countervailing power that enables this majority to reconfigure the market.

8. A countervailing power should not only reorganize the market to distribute income more evenly, but it must also develop market rules to counteract the trends of globalization and technological innovation that tend to benefit the one percenters and cost the lower classes their jobs.

ANALYSIS

Key Takeaway 1

There is no such thing as the free market.

Analysis

The free market is a myth that masks the reality of how the rules of the economic game are fixed and distracts attention away from the possibility of reorganizing the economy in a way that works for the majority of people. The major economic debate between Republicans and Democrats tends to be about how much the government should interfere in the workings of the market. Framed this way, the debate is already deeply deceiving. It positions the government as an unnatural, problematic entity distorting a system of naturally operating forces. But the free market does not exist without a government that creates and enforces the rules by which it operates. In fact, there is no economic system, no economy period, without these rules.

The idea of a free market has also been historically described as laissez-faire economics, a French term meaning letting go. The idea originated in the Enlightenment thinking of the 18th century. Philosophers were preoccupied with the idea of nature and natural rights, which they saw as harmonious, just, and self-regulating. For this reason, they sought to create systems that did away with artificial constraints and returned to the spontaneity of the natural order [1]. This thinking has a distinctly moral bent to it. Nature is by definition virtuous and right. Anything that alters it is damaging. Laissez-faire imagines a kind of perfect world, an Eden of economic activity in which the market imitates the harmonious, self-regulating order of the natural world. Adam Smith, an English philosopher and economist, was one of the major thinkers in this tradition [2]. For him, a laissez-faire system freed the market from constraining laws, restored order, and activated the potential for growth.

Key Takeaway 2

It is no coincidence that those who praise the free market are the moneyed interests who benefit most from this system.

Analysis

Since there is no such thing as an economy without rules, the free market really allows certain interests to establish a certain set of rules by which they profit. It is not a deregulated economy so much as a re-regulated one, with laws that allow Wall Street to speculate, for instance, on risky and lucrative bets, or that allow banks to push mortgages on people who cannot afford them. These rules obviously enhance the income and wealth of a tiny fraction of the US population, the so-called one percenters. Naturally, they have no inclination to introduce a different set of rules that would rein in the activity that makes their economic power possible.

There is enormous rhetorical deception at play in the way the term free market is thrown around. It plays to deeply held beliefs in the US about freedom itself. Those who continue to praise the free market and demonize big government are effectively interested in keeping the majority of the people in the dark about what these terms really mean. The ignorance of the majority works in favor of the wealthy minority who are able to hide their real intentions behind this simplistic insistence on freedom.

Key Takeaway 3

Economic and political power are deeply connected. As moneyed interests gain dominance over the economy, they increase their influence over government, which in turn allows them to continue growing their wealth and entrenching their economic power.

Analysis

A democracy is intended to reflect the values and interests of the majority of citizens. Over the last couple of decades, however, wealthy individuals and corporations have gained increasing power over government itself and, by extension, over government decisions about the rules of the market. This does not generally happen in overtly corrupt or immoral ways like giving and receiving bribes. Instead, government officials, including politicians, regulatory heads, and judges, are influenced by moneyed interests. They receive substantial campaign contributions or the promise of comfy jobs on Wall Street or in lobbying firms at the end of their tenure in government. The Supreme Court's 2010 decision in *Citizens United v. Federal Election Commission* that granted large corporations the ability to finance political advertising campaigns is one example of how this has been allowed to happen.

In this way, the wealthy few use their economic power to override the interests of average citizens. It is not surprising that their influence over government then opens up a path for them to continue controlling the market in ways that enhance their wealth. This sounds like something of a conspiracy in which select people in the US, from positions of power both inside and outside of government, get together to hatch unethical schemes. In fact, these people are simply operating according to their rational self-interest. They are not evil so much as predictably selfish, and they get away with their behavior because the majority fails to oppose them.

Key Takeaway 4

The influence of the wealthy on the economy and politics undermines the trust on which capitalism depends. Lack of trust further damages the political and economic system as people become cynical, avoid reasonable financial risks, and start cheating in order to get by.

Analysis

Cynicism and apathy are rampant in US politics today. Political rhetoric disparages those who are insiders or part of the Washington establishment and favors outsiders who are not part of what many perceive to be a corrupt system. This is no doubt why non-politicians, like Donald Trump, Ben Carson, and Carly Fiorina, have done so well in the 2016 Republican primary polls [3]. Frustration with the status quo has led people in the US to distrust government and politicians alike.

Voter turnout has also been markedly weak in recent years. Compared to other Western democracies, the US sees a fairly low representation of its citizens at the polls [4]. This, too, is a mark of the widespread distrust and disbelief in the current system. People do not think their vote has the power to change anything, or they do not believe the available representatives will fairly represent their interests. But this is a dangerous state of affairs because it makes it exceedingly difficult to actually change or improve the way things work, both in government and in the market. Moreover, as long as average people do not feel capable of creating a system that works for the majority, moneyed interests will continue to hold sway, deepening the cynicism and distrust.

Key Takeaway 5

The notion that people earn what they are worth is a fallacy as it disregards the political institutions that define the market and determine worth. It also encourages people to think there is nothing they can do to improve their situation.

Analysis

The idea that people earn what they are worth is a slippery notion by which a person's income is interpreted to suggest qualities about their character and worth as a human being. For instance, Republicans often rail against welfare programs and big government initiatives for encouraging people to be lazy, unproductive, and parasitic. The implication is that people at the bottom of the income bracket are there because of their own moral failings. This thinking encourages the idea that big government is bad because it does not give people incentives for improving their poor work ethic. On the other end of the spectrum, individuals who amass tremendous wealth are praised for their industry and intelligence. Belief in the free market dictates that these people are not selfish or greedy. They have simply earned what they are worth and they deserve the luxuries that come with their earnings.

But this thinking does not make sense when, increasingly, people can work full-time jobs, sometimes two or more jobs, and still not make enough money to create a reasonable standard of living for their family. Similarly, it does not make sense that the rich who inherit wealth somehow deserve or have earned money that they never worked for. On the contrary, they got lucky through an accident of birth.

Key Takeaway 6

The increasing power and influence of the US upper class has come at the expense of the declining power of the working and middle classes. The main problem is not economic, but political.

Analysis

In political debates, the discussion tends to revolve around how much the wealthy should pay and what taxes should be. Predictably, Republicans want to keep taxes to a minimum while Democrats want to see the wealthy pay more. However, this discussion, often focused on economic redistribution, is just a Band-Aid. It does not get to the root of the problem, which is who controls government and sets the rules by which the market operates. A market that is responsive to the needs of a wealthy minority cannot create a fair and prosperous society for the majority. People must understand this relationship between politics and economics. Instead of expressing apathy for the way money has corrupted politics, they must take back control of the US political system and the government for the people.

This is a fervent call to citizenship and to the renewal of democracy, a kind of rebirth in the founding principles of the United States, a return to the roots of the US political system. It is the opposite of indifference. It is active engagement and faith in the possibility of a better, more equitable society. In other words, understanding US political and economic failings does not have to lead to further cynicism and apathy. Rather, it should be the cause for a political awakening that unites people and mobilizes them to take back power over their government.

Key Takeaway 7

The growing divide in US society is not between Republicans and Democrats, but between the establishment and everyone else, the wealthy and the struggling majority. Ordinary people must establish a countervailing power that enables this majority to reconfigure the market.

Analysis

It is commonplace in the 21st century to point out how divided the US has become, how ideological, and how partisan in its disputes and divisions. Hatred between Republicans and Democrats is particularly sharp. Both view the other as the enemy, as a force for destruction in US society. However, this ideological battle obscures the greater division that plagues political and economic spheres, the growing divide between the very wealthy and the majority of Americans. In fact, this problem could be something that unites working and middle class people across the ideological divide. It could bring Democrats and Republicans together to reclaim political power and reorganize the market.

In this light, ideological controversy over noneconomic issues becomes something of a distraction from the central problem and partisanship itself exacerbates the situation insofar as it keeps the majority from coming together against the wealthy minority. Increasingly, people voice disgust with the Wall Street-Washington alliance [5]. The question is whether their frustration with moneyed interests can sufficiently override partisanship and party resentments to create a unified front. As the inequality gap continues to widen, it seems inevitable that sheer necessity will eventually drive people to oppose and correct the current system.

Key Takeaway 8

A countervailing power should not only reorganize the market to distribute income more evenly, but it must also develop market rules to counteract the trends of globalization and technological innovation that tend to benefit the one percenters and cost the lower classes their jobs.

Analysis

The problems that face the US economy are multiple and complex. They involve not only the problematic political power of Wall Street, large corporations, and wealthy individuals, but also the enormous shifts underway in the global economy. Cheap labor overseas and disruptive, breakthrough technologies are taking jobs away from US workers. A long-term vision for a sustainable future must factor in all these dynamics. Although job loss sounds devastating, it does not have to be. Alternate visions for how the economy could be organized, put forth by thinkers like Thomas Paine, point to different options. These require creative thinking and significant changes in the organization of the US economy, but unprecedented economic trouble calls for unprecedented transformation.

Though suffering and economic injustice are tragic, there is something exciting about the breakthroughs and ideas this crisis precipitates. The situation highlights the sense in which deep-seated problems can become a source for renewal and rebirth, for a return to a nation's basic principles but also reinterpretation and reexamination of them in light of new challenges and the evolving dynamics of a global order. Pessimism here transforms into optimism, and frustration becomes a spur for innovation.

AUTHOR'S STYLE

Saving Capitalism is divided into three parts. Each part is further divided into multiple chapters. This organization offers a coherent, natural progression of Reich's argument, from a discussion of how the US economic system is organized to an analysis of the faults and dangers of the system to a vision of how it can be corrected. Though the book tackles daunting ideas in economic and political theory, Reich's language is clear, informative, and accessible. He draws frequently on concrete examples from a wide range of industries to illustrate his arguments, rendering the ideas comprehensible even to readers who are not well versed in economics.

Reich's style is direct and straightforward. Though he is clearly concerned with the state of the US economic system and frustrated by the forces that have distorted it, his language never veers into excessive or sensational expressions of anger. Rather, his stated intention is to correct gross misconceptions about the market and equip readers with the knowledge and understanding necessary to act on the problems at hand. This leads him, at times, to emphasize and repeat his overriding concerns. To some extent, the repetition is helpful as it helps drive Reich's thesis home, but it can also start to feel wordy and unnecessary. On the whole, however, the book is eminently instructive, offering both an informed critique of the market and a clear set of suggestions for what can be done to change things for the better.

AUTHOR'S PERSPECTIVE

Reich is Chancellor's Professor of Public Policy at Richard and Rhoda Goldman School of Public Policy at the University of California, Berkeley, and the author of 14 books, including *The Work of Nations*, *Supercapitalism,* and *Aftershock.* He is a senior fellow at the Blum Center for Developing Economies, a fellow of the American Academy of Arts and Sciences, and has served in three national administrations, most recently as secretary of labor under President Bill Clinton.

Saving Capitalism is motivated by Reich's perception of a widespread and dangerous misconception about the so-called free market. He writes in order to correct this misconception and shift the debate in a way that can realistically address the economic and political problems that concern him. His tone is cautionary, but ultimately optimistic, as he believes that accurate information can motivate people to work together to find sustainable solutions. He even outlines what some of these solutions could look like, underscoring the idea that an alternative to the troublesome status quo is entirely within reach.

~~~~~~ END OF INSTAREAD~~~~~~

RESOURCES

1. Fine, Sidney. *Laissez Faire and the General-Welfare State*. United States: The University of Michigan Press, 1964. http://www.amazon.com/Laissez-Faire-General-Welfare-State-Paperbacks/dp/0472060864
2. Smith, Adam. *The Wealth of Nations.* England: Methuen & Co., Ltd, 1776. http://www.amazon.com/The-Wealth-Nations-Bantam-Classics/dp/0553585975
3. Kamarck, Elaine. "Why Non-Politicians Are So Popular," Newsweek.com, accessed Nov. 5, 2015, http://www.newsweek.com/why-non-politicians-are-so-popular-374808.
4. Desilver, Drew. "US voter turnout trails most developed countries," Pew Research.com, accessed Nov. 5, 2015, http://www.pewresearch.org/fact-tank/2015/05/06/u-s-voter-turnout-trails-most-developed-countries/
5. Madison, Lucy. "Obama: 'Occupy Wall Street' reflects 'broad-based frustration'." CBSNews.com, accessed Nov. 5, 2015,

http://www.cbsnews.com/news/obama-occupy-wall-street-reflects-broad-based-frustration/

Made in the USA
Middletown, DE
02 February 2016